POULTRY FOR BEGINNER

Guide To Raising Healthy seam, Boosting Egg Production, And Maximizing Profits With Proven Strategies

Holden bodhi

Contents

CHAPTER ONE 9
- An Overview Of Layer Farming In Poultry 9
  - An Overview Of Layer Farming For Poultry....................11
  - Advantages And Difficulties 14
  - Important Phrases And Ideas 16

CHAPTER TWO..19
- Organizing Your Farm For Poultry Layers 19
  - Site Selection And Design..19
  - Financial Planning And Budgeting 22
  - Regulatory And Legal Aspects 25

CHAPTER THREE 29
- Selecting The Appropriate Breed 29
  - Well-Liked Layer Breeds..29
  - Features Of The Breed And Egg Production 32
  - Breed Selection Dependent On Local Climate................35

CHAPTER FOUR..39
- Organizing Your Housing For Poultry...................................39
  - Different Housing System Types......................................39
  - Plan And Airflow 42
  - Boxes For Nesting And Perches 46

CHAPTER FIVE 49
- Nutrition And Feeding 49
  - Essential Nutritional Needs...49
  - Feed And Supplement Types 51

Feeding Plans And Administration 54

CHAPTER SIX 57

Typical Poultry Illnesses And How To Avoid Them 57

Overview Of Poultry Illnesses 57

Medication And Vaccination 60

Using Biosecurity To Stop Outbreaks... 63

CHAPTER SEVEN 67

Production And Handling Of Eggs.. 67

Knowing The Cycles Of Egg-Laying.. 67

crucial stages of the egg-laying process 67

Affecting Factors For Egg Production.. 68

Gathering And Treating Eggs 70

Tools And Methods For Gathering Eggs 70

Storage As Well As Quality Assurance 72

CHAPTER EIGHT 75

Preserving The Welfare Of Poultry.. 75

Keeping An Eye On Behavior And Health................................ 75

Bringing In Environmental Enhancement 77

Handling Injuries And Stress... 79

CHAPTER NINE.. 83

Sanitation And Waste Management In Layer Farming Of Poultry 83

Techniques For Discarding Waste... 83

Facilities Cleaning And Disinfection... 86

Recycling And Composting Trash.. 90

CHAPTER TEN 95

  Putting Your Eggs On The Market And Selling Them 95

    Finding The Right Target Markets 95

    Strategies For Pricing 98

    Distribution And Packaging 101

CHAPTER ELEVEN 105

  Developing And Growing Your Farm 105

    Making Growth Plans 105

    Including New Equipment And Facilities 107

    Overseeing Bigger Flocks And Activities 110

    Conclusion 113

    Beginner's Guide To Poultry Layer Farming: Important Things To Know 117

Copyright © 2024 by Holden bodhi

All rights reserved.

No part of this publication may be reproduced, distributed, or transmitted in any form or by any means, including photocopying, recording, or other electronic or mechanical methods, without the prior written permission of the publisher, except in the case of brief quotations embodied in critical reviews and certain other non commercial uses permitted by copyright law.

DISCLAIMER

The information provided in this book, is intended for educational and informational purposes only. The content is based on research, personal experiences, and general knowledge about farming. It is not intended to substitute professional advice or expert consultation. Readers are encouraged to seek professional guidance when implementing any practices or techniques discussed in this book.

The author and publisher make no representations or warranties of any kind regarding the accuracy, applicability, or completeness of the contents of this book. Any reliance you place on such information is strictly at your own risk. The author and publisher shall not be held liable for any damages, losses, or injuries resulting from the use of the information provided.

Additionally, the author does not endorse, recommend, or affiliate with any individual, product, service, website, organization, or brand mentioned or referenced in this book. Any such references are solely for informational purposes, and no warranty or guarantee is implied. The inclusion of these references does not imply any endorsement or partnership by the author.

By reading this book, you acknowledge and accept that the author and publisher are not responsible for any consequences arising from your use of the information provided.

CHAPTER ONE

An Overview Of Layer Farming In Poultry

A specialized subset of chicken farming with an emphasis on egg production is called poultry layer farming. Layer farming is centered on hens that have been particularly bred to produce eggs efficiently, as opposed to grill farming, which is focused on rearing birds for meat. There are many sizes at which this kind of farming may be carried out, ranging from modest backyard installations to massive commercial operations. It is an essential component of the agricultural sector and a major global source of nutrition and protein for humans.

Maintaining steady and superior egg production is the fundamental goal of layer farming. This calls for careful control of the food, housing, and well-being of the birds. Known as their laying cycle, layer hens are typically reared for a particular amount of time during which they lay eggs. To guarantee maximum yield, they are often replaced with younger chickens once their productivity starts to fall.

The Value of Layer Farming for Poultry

Layer farming of poultry is essential to nutrition and food security. Eggs are a very nutrient-dense meal that includes important proteins, vitamins, and minerals. They are also reasonably priced in comparison to other animal protein sources, which enables a wide range of people to have access to them. Additionally, the industry makes a substantial economic contribution via trade and employment generation.

Beginning with Farming Poultry Layers

Establishing a layer farm for chickens needs significant thought and preparation. Prospective farmers must determine the size of their enterprise and evaluate their resources, including land, money, and experience. Furthermore, in order to guarantee productive and sustainable farming, they need to be knowledgeable about local laws and best practices.

An Overview Of Layer Farming For Poultry

Different Kinds of Layer Systems

Systems for layer farming may be roughly divided into three categories: free-range, cage-free, and typical cage systems.

1. Conventional Cage Systems: In these systems, chickens are housed in spacious barns in tiny cages. Although this technique makes it possible to harvest eggs in a high-density and effective manner, its effects on animal welfare have drawn criticism. The mobility and natural behaviors of the chickens may be restricted in caged settings.

2. Cage-Free Systems: Hens are housed in spacious, open barns with plenty of room to roam about, lay eggs in nesting boxes, and partake in their natural activities, such as taking dust baths. Comparing cage-free systems to regular cages, the goal is to increase animal well-being.

3. Hens kept in free-range settings have access to the outdoors, which enables them to graze and behave naturally. Although this method may need more resources, it is often chosen because of its alleged improvements to egg quality and animal welfare.

Methods of Production

The management strategies and overall profitability of the farm are greatly impacted by the production technique selection. In any system, elements including environmental controls, disease management, and feed formulation are essential.

1. Feed Management: Keeping hens healthy and producing eggs requires proper nourishment. Proteins, vitamins, and minerals are among the vital components that should be included in a balanced diet.

2. Health Management: To lower the risk of illness, preventative health measures are crucial, such as immunizations and biosecurity procedures. Regular monitoring and health examinations are also essential.

3. Environmental Controls: To ensure the comfort and productivity of the hens, it is essential to maintain ideal environmental conditions, including temperature, humidity, and ventilation.

Financial Aspects

A crucial component of layer farming for chickens is economic viability. The price of eggs is determined by market pricing as well as the initial setup and continuing operating costs. Profitability requires both an awareness of market dynamics and efficient cost control.

Advantages And Difficulties
Advantages of Layer Farming for Poultry

1. High Egg Production: Throughout their laying cycle, layer hens may produce a huge number of eggs due to their high productivity. Because of this, layer farming may be quite profitable if done correctly.

2. Nutritional Value: Rich in protein and other nutrients, eggs help customers eat a healthier diet. An egg market that is stable may result from this need.

3. Economic chances: Selling eggs may bring in money for poultry layer farms, and the sector can provide job chances.

4. Adaptability: Depending on available resources and market circumstances, poultry layer farming may be flexible and implemented at different sizes and systems.

Difficulties in Raising Poultry Layers

1. Disease Control: A number of illnesses may affect poultry, which can have an effect on both productivity and health. It is essential to put into practice efficient disease management techniques.

2. Biosecurity Risks: It might be difficult to keep the flock safe from outside dangers and to make sure biosecurity protocols are followed. Disease outbreaks and contamination may have serious effects.

3. Market Variations: Demand in the market, feed pricing, and level of competition may all affect egg prices. Financial management and meticulous planning are necessary to control these swings.

4. Animal wellbeing: There is an increasing concern about ensuring the well-being of hens, especially in systems where they are confined. Adherence to animal welfare norms and protocols is becoming more and more crucial.

Important Phrases And Ideas
Hens in Layers

The purpose of layer hen breeding is to maximize egg production. Successful layer farming requires an understanding of their life cycle, nutritional requirements, and health requirements.

Cycle of Laying

The time when chickens are actively laying eggs is known as the laying cycle. After around 18 weeks, they usually go through this cycle until they are about 72 weeks old, at which point their egg production may start to decrease.

Formulation of Feed

Feed formulation entails supplying the chickens with nutritious, well-balanced food. Both general health and good egg production are supported by a well-formulated diet.

Biosecurity

The term "biosecurity" describes the precautions used in chicken farms to stop the entry and spread of illness. This covers procedures like maintaining hygiene, imposing a quarantine, and limiting access to the farm.

Metrics for Egg Production

A chicken layer farm's performance must be assessed using metrics including egg production rate, feed conversion ratio, and egg quality. These measurements aid in determining the operation's productivity and efficiency.

CHAPTER TWO

Organizing Your Farm For Poultry Layers

Site Selection And Design

Recognizing the Needs of Poultry Layer Farming

The success of your chicken layer farm depends on the location you choose. Start by assessing the basic requirements of your layers, such as the availability of clean water, space, and ventilation. Dry, well-ventilated conditions are necessary for poultry layers to be healthy and productive. Pick a place with plenty of room for sheltering, feeding, and disposing of waste.

Evaluation of Environmental and Soil Factors

The way your farm is run is greatly influenced by the environmental factors and soil quality of the location you have selected. Make sure the ground drains properly to avoid floods and waterlogging, which may harm your hens' health. To reduce the chance of contamination, the location should be far from places with high traffic or industrial sectors.

Close to Markets and Resources

Think about how close you are to markets, veterinary care, and feed providers, among other important things. Reducing transportation expenses and guaranteeing prompt access to essential goods and services may be achieved by residing near these resources. In addition, assess the accessibility of the local roads for the transportation and distribution of your goods.

Creating the Farm's Layout

Optimizing the arrangement leads to increased production and efficiency. Start by arranging your chicken buildings so that enough natural light and ventilation can pass through them. Create distinct spaces for feeding, watering, and disposing of garbage in order to keep things hygienic and boost productivity. If you want to increase the size of your flock in the future, provide room for growth.

Making Waste Management Plans

Keeping your layers' surroundings tidy and healthy depends on efficient waste management. Make sure your farm has enough space for composting and trash disposal. Putting a waste management strategy into practice protects your flock's health and productivity while reducing the negative effects on the environment.

Measures for Safety and Security

Make sure that the security features in your farm architecture shield your layers from intruders and predators. Surveillance systems, safe housing, and fencing may assist protect your investment and guarantee the security of your birds.

Financial Planning And Budgeting
Calculating Startup Expenses

Setting up your chicken layer farm successfully requires accurate budgeting. Start by calculating the start-up costs, which include expenditures for purchasing equipment, building chicken homes, acquiring land, and investing in a flock of birds. Remember to include in expenses for utilities, veterinary care, and nutrition.

infrastructure and land costs

Infrastructure and land may come at a high cost. Look around and evaluate costs in various places to identify the greatest choice for your money. When constructing chicken houses, feed storage facilities, and waste management facilities, take into account the price of labor and building supplies. Don't forget to account for the installation costs of essential services like power and water.

Tools and Materials

Purchasing top-notch tools and supplies is essential to your farm's smooth functioning. Set aside money for things like waterers, feeds, heaters, and tools for collecting eggs. Your financial strategy should take possible upgrades and routine maintenance into account.

Function-related Costs

The continuous expenditures of labor, feed, veterinary care, and utilities are included in operational expenses. Create a thorough budget that accounts for these ongoing expenses to guarantee the longevity of your farm. Maintaining profitability and making necessary adjustments to your business may be achieved by closely monitoring and controlling these expenditures.

Income Forecasts

Assess prospective earnings by calculating the anticipated production and cost of eggs. Examine current egg market pricing and take into account variables like local demand and competition that might impact your sales.

To determine the profitability of your farm, make a financial estimate that includes expected revenue and contrasts it with your outlays.

Emergency Preparedness

Have a contingency fund put up to cover unforeseen costs and emergencies. You can better handle unanticipated expenses like equipment maintenance and disease outbreaks with the aid of this fund.

By keeping some money aside, you can deal with problems without endangering the health of your farm.

Regulatory And Legal Aspects

Recognizing Local Laws

Prior to beginning a layer farm, it is crucial to comprehend and abide by zoning rules and local ordinances. Examine the particular requirements—such as licenses, permits, and land use restrictions—that your community may have for raising chicken. For businesses to operate lawfully and to stay out of trouble with the law or penalties, compliance with these standards is essential.

Licenses and Permits

Acquire the licenses and permissions needed for raising chickens. These might include commercial licenses, environmental permissions, and agricultural permits. Before starting your business, make sure you have all the necessary paperwork by getting in touch with the local government offices or agricultural organizations.

Standards for Animal Welfare

Respect the guidelines established by regulatory bodies on animal care. These guidelines include things like your layers' health care, food habits, and living circumstances. In addition to promoting the health of your flock, according to these rules can be necessary in order to get certification and gain access to markets.

Rules Regarding the Environment

Respect environmental laws pertaining to pollution prevention, water use, and waste management. Put in place measures to reduce the environmental effect of your farm, such as appropriate waste disposal and water conservation. To keep your procedures compliant with evolving rules, examine and update them on a regular basis.

Regulations for Health and Safety

To safeguard your layers as well as your employees, make sure your farm complies with health and safety requirements. This entails providing a secure workplace, offering appropriate training for managing chickens, and putting policies in place to stop the spread of illnesses. To ensure compliance, regular inspections and adherence to safety procedures are crucial.

Liability and Insurance

If you want to safeguard your farm from potential dangers including property damage, liability claims, and revenue loss, you should think about getting insurance coverage. Insurance may help you handle possible risks and unanticipated situations by offering financial stability and peace of mind. To get the right coverage for your unique circumstances, speak with insurance pros.

CHAPTER THREE

Selecting The Appropriate Breed

Well-Liked Layer Breeds

Choosing the appropriate breed is one of the most important choices you will make when starting a layer farm for poultry. The production and general profitability of your farm may be greatly impacted by the breed you choose. Every breed has distinct traits that affect egg yield, egg quality, and the birds' ability to adapt to different surroundings.

1. RI Red

The Rhode Island Red is well recognized for its resilience and abundant egg-laying ability. Because of its adaptability to different environments, this variety is suitable for both small-scale and commercial farming. Large brown eggs and the ability to continue laying in less-than-ideal circumstances are two characteristics of Rhode Island Red chickens. Many novices choose them because of their minimal care requirements and ability to withstand sickness.

2. Leghorn

Another popular breed is the leghorn, which is well-known for producing large amounts of eggs. Because of their capacity to provide a large quantity of white eggs, they are effective layers and are often used in commercial egg production. Though they do better in warmer areas, leghorns are adaptable and active in a variety of settings. They are a great option for those who want to maximize productivity because of their versatility and high production rates.

3. Sussex

The Sussex breed is prized for its ability to function as a meat bird in addition to an egg layer. They are well-suited for backyard and small-scale farming because of their placid temperament and good egg production. Large brown eggs are produced by resilient Sussex hens, although they do need more attention than Rhode Island Reds or Leghorns. They are a flexible option for novices due to their adaptability to various conditions.

4. Australia Lorp

Australorps are well-known for their outstanding ability to lay eggs, especially big brown eggs, which they consistently produce. This breed is excellent for novices because of its reputation for gentleness and versatility.

Furthermore, australorps are renowned for being able to withstand a wide range of weather conditions, making them adaptable to both hot and cold settings. Many poultry producers favor them because of their easy handling and consistent egg output.

5. Plymouth Rock

Plymouth Rocks are a well-liked option for home chicken raising because of their amiable nature and consistent egg output. They are distinguished by their beautiful striped plumage and lay medium- to large-sized brown eggs. This breed is a good choice in a variety of climes because of its reputation for resilience to many environmental circumstances. They are a great option for beginning farmers because of their peaceful disposition and good egg-laying ability.

Features Of The Breed And Egg Production

To choose the best layer chickens for your farm, it is crucial to comprehend the characteristics of each breed. The right breed of bird for your requirements will depend on a number of factors, including temperament, egg size, and productivity.

1. Production of Eggs

Different breeds produce eggs at different rates. Leghorns, for example, are renowned for their large egg production, often yielding over 300 eggs annually. Conversely, breeds like Sussex are prized for their quality and consistency even if they may lay fewer eggs. It might be useful to know each breed's egg production capability in order to choose a breed that best suits your farming objectives.

2. Egg Dimensions and Grade

Breeds might differ in the size and quality of eggs they produce. While certain varieties—like the Australorp—are recognized for laying enormous eggs, other types could lay medium-sized eggs. The eggs' quality may also vary, as can the yolk color and shell strength. Selecting a breed that satisfies your requirements for quality is essential to guarantee marketability and customer pleasure.

3. Behaviour and Attitude

The breed's disposition influences how easy or difficult it is to manage a flock. While certain breeds, like the Plymouth Rock, are more laid-back and manageable, others could be more energetic and need more room. You may decide how well a breed will fit into your agricultural setup and how much time you will need to devote to their care by taking into account the breed's disposition.

4. Hardiness and Adaptability

The degree to which different breeds can adapt to various habitats and climates varies. Leghorns, for instance, could be more suited for warmer regions, while Rhode Island Reds are renowned for their resilience in a variety of settings. Evaluating each breed's degree of adaptation and hardiness can assist you in choosing one that will flourish in your particular environment.

Breed Selection Dependent On Local Climate

The health and production of your flock depend on your choice of breed, which should be matched to the environment in your area. The degree to which different breeds can withstand variations in temperature, humidity, and other environmental conditions varies.

1. Considerations for Cold Climates

Breeds with greater resistance to cold are better suited for regions with severe winters and low temperatures. Because of their thick feathers and ability to withstand cold conditions, breeds like the Rhode Island Red and the Australorp have shown excellent performance in colder areas. It is possible for these breeds to regularly produce eggs even in the cold.

2. Considerations for a Hot Climate

It is important to choose breeds that can withstand heat stress in hot and humid conditions. The capacity of leghorns and Plymouth Rocks to acclimatize to warmer climates and continue laying eggs in the face of elevated temperatures is well recognized. Providing sufficient shade and ventilation may also aid in these breeds' success in hot climates.

3. Rainfall and Humidity

The health and production of layer hens may be impacted by high humidity and frequent rains. Breeds best adapted to such settings include those less susceptible to respiratory problems and feather damage from humid circumstances. The effects of heavy humidity and rain on your flock may be lessened by making sure your housing and ventilation are adequate.

4. Seasonal Differences

When choosing a breed, take into account the seasonal differences in your location. Certain breeds may be able to adjust better to seasonal variations and continue to produce eggs consistently all year round. Knowing how various breeds behave in different seasons can help you choose a breed that will consistently produce eggs throughout the year, even with seasonal variations.

CHAPTER FOUR

Organizing Your Housing For Poultry

Different Housing System Types

For layer hens to be healthy and productive, adequate housing must be set up. There are several housing system kinds to take into account, each with unique benefits and specifications.

1. Conventional Cooperative System

For small-scale chicken growers, the conventional coop system is often their first option. These coops usually have a straightforward form and are constructed of wood. Typically, they include standard characteristics including nesting boxes, roosting bars, and sufficient ventilation. Conventional coops are quite simple to construct and maintain, and they may be tailored to the amount of layers you want to keep. If handled well, they may provide hens with a pleasant lifestyle and are perfect for backyard flocks.

2. A-Type Apartments

Because of its effective use of space and ventilation, A-frame housing is a popular option. This design is similar to an A-frame building, with the roof sloping downward towards the sides. In addition to assisting with water drainage, the sloping roof may provide shade. Enclosed spaces are a common feature of A-frame buildings, shielding the hens from inclement weather and predators. They work well in pasture-based systems where hens may graze since they are generally mobile.

3. Cages for Batteries

The main use for battery cages is in industrial chicken production. These are big, tiered cages that can hold many chickens each. Battery cages' layout facilitates effective space utilization and makes feeding, watering, and cleaning procedures simpler. However, since battery cages provide little room for normal behaviors, there are worries about the well-being of chickens housed in them. Many areas now need to amend their regulations in order to enhance the circumstances inside these systems.

4. Unrestricted Systems

Hens in free-range systems are allowed to wander outside of their housing. These systems usually include of an outside space where the hens may graze in addition to a barn or shed where they can find refuge and deposit their eggs. Better living circumstances and support for natural behaviors are provided by free-range housing for birds. To protect the hens' health and safety, nevertheless, it might necessitate more stringent management techniques and a larger area requirement.

5. Aircraft Systems

A more contemporary method of keeping chickens is via aviary systems, especially in larger-scale companies. Hens may wander between levels in these multi-level systems, which mimic a more natural setting. More room is available for mobility in aviaries, which may also include amenities like perches, scratching places, and nesting spaces. They are made to support the health and welfare of the chickens when handling bigger flocks.

Plan And Airflow

Keeping layer hens in a healthy environment is largely dependent on the layout and ventilation of their house. An appropriately designed home guarantees the birds' comfort, efficiency, and functionality.

1. Design-Related Issues

The design of housing for chickens should put comfort, protection, and simplicity of management first. For every hen, the housing should have enough area for her to roam about, eat, and lay eggs. To avoid trash accumulation and maintain hygiene, the layout should make cleaning and maintenance simple. In order to defend against predators and inclement weather, think about adding features like safe doors and windows.

2. Systems of Ventilation

To keep the atmosphere in the chicken house healthy, proper ventilation is necessary. Proper ventilation lowers the risk of respiratory disorders and other health difficulties by regulating humidity, temperature, and air quality. There are several types of ventilation systems available:

• Natural Ventilation: This system depends on air moving naturally via open vents, windows, and roof openings. It may be useful in preserving temperature control and air quality and is often used in smaller-scale applications. Careful planning is necessary for natural ventilation to provide sufficient airflow and avoid drafts.

• Mechanical Ventilation: To regulate airflow and maintain the ideal environmental conditions, mechanical ventilation systems make use of fans and other devices. Larger companies often employ this technology because it offers more accurate temperature and humidity control. For best effects, mechanical and natural ventilation may be mixed.

• Tunnel Ventilation: This particular kind of mechanical ventilation includes forcing a fast-moving airstream through the chicken house. The chickens are kept in a cozy atmosphere thanks to this system's rapid removal of heat and moisture. Large-scale operations often use tunnel ventilation, which may be useful in preserving steady conditions.

3. Control of Temperature

Layer chicken production and health depend on the poultry housing's temperature being kept at the right level. Heating systems, insulation, and ventilation may all help regulate temperature. Insulation may aid in heat retention in cold areas, minimizing the need for additional heating. Shade and ventilation are crucial in hot climes to avoid overheating.

4. Controlling Humidity

It is important to monitor and regulate the humidity levels in the chicken house to avoid moisture accumulation and the development of dangerous diseases. In addition to raising the risk of illness, high humidity may cause respiratory problems. Maintaining a healthy environment for the hens may be achieved by controlling humidity levels through frequent cleaning and proper ventilation.

Boxes For Nesting And Perches

Poultry housing must have nesting boxes and perches because these provide the hens with comfortable areas to relax and lay eggs.

1. Nesting Containers

Nesting boxes provide hens with a cozy and secluded area to lay their eggs, which is essential for egg production. The layout and arrangement of nesting boxes might affect the hens' well-being and output.

• Size & Dimensions: Every nesting box has to be big enough to fit a hen in comfort. A standard size is around 12 by 12 inches, however the breed and size of the chickens might affect this. The nesting box's height should be low enough to provide the hens with easy access.

• Construction and Material: Wood, plastic, and metal are some of the materials that may be used to make nesting boxes. The material must be simple to maintain and clean. To provide the chickens with a cozy and clean environment, think about adding bedding materials like hay, straw, or wood shavings.

• Location: To encourage hens to utilize nesting boxes, position them in a peaceful, dark corner of the poultry house. The boxes must be situated at a height that prevents other chickens from disturbing them and should be readily accessible. Multiple nesting boxes might lessen stress and rivalry among the flock.

2. Perches

Because they provide the hens a place to relax and roost, perches are vital to the health of layer chickens. The location and shape of the perch may improve the birds' comfort and well-being.

• Size and Dimensions: Hens should be able to grab and rest securely on perches that are broad enough. The diameter of a normal perch is between 1.5 and 2 inches. The chickens' sizes and the layout of the housing should be taken into consideration while determining the height of the perches.

• Material and Construction: Wood, metal, or plastic may be used to make stools. It should be simple to clean and have a long lifespan. Think of using materials that won't cause the chickens any pain or harm and are cozy for their feet.

• Positioning: It is best to provide perches at different heights so that hens may choose their favorite spot to rest. To avoid contamination and provide a calm resting place, the perches should be placed apart from feeding areas and nesting boxes. Make sure the perches are firmly fixed and strong enough to hold the hens' weight.

CHAPTER FIVE

Nutrition And Feeding

Essential Nutritional Needs
Overview of Nutrition for Poultry

Knowing the fundamental dietary needs of hens in chicken layer farming is essential to maintaining their well-being and output. A well-balanced diet is necessary for layers to maintain their general health, maintain their feathers, and produce eggs. In addition to increasing egg supply, a healthy diet lowers the risk of illness and increases egg quality.

Proteins, Carbohydrates, and Fats are macronutrients.

Growth, egg production, and tissue healing all depend on proteins. Generally speaking, layers' diets should include 16–18% protein. In chicken feed, fish meal, canola meal, and soybean meal are the main sources of protein. Grain products like maize and wheat provide carbohydrates, which supply the energy required for everyday tasks and the development of eggs. Poultry feed contains lipids, such as animal or vegetable oils, to increase energy levels and facilitate the absorption of fat-soluble vitamins.

Minerals and vitamins are micronutrients.

Minerals and vitamins are essential for the health of chickens. Vitamins A, D, and E are essential for healthy bones, eyesight, and reproductive function. Mineral needs include phosphorus, which combines with calcium to support bone formation, and calcium, which is necessary for robust eggshells. Enzyme activity and metabolic processes also depend on trace elements like manganese and zinc. To avoid deficiencies, a balanced poultry feed will include these micronutrients in the right proportions.

Water Consumption and Its Significance

An essential part of the poultry diet is water. As clean, fresh water is essential for digestion, nutrition absorption, and egg production, layers must have regular access to it. Low water intake may cause health problems, low egg production, and a reduction in feed consumption. Layer farming requires certain procedures, like securing a steady supply of water and periodically testing the quality of the water.

Feed And Supplement Types
Feeds for Commercial Layers

The nutritional requirements of laying hens are satisfied by commercially produced layer meals. These foods are available in pellet, crumble, and mash formats. Because it is more convenient and produces less waste, pelletized feed is widely used. More feeding flexibility is possible with crumbles and mash, particularly if layers have particular nutritional requirements. By choosing premium commercial feeds from reliable vendors, you can be confident that hens are fed a balanced diet that promotes maximum egg production.

Feeds Made of Grains

One of the mainstays of chicken nutrition is grain-based feed. Common grains used in layer rations include corn, wheat, barley, and oats. To satisfy the hens' complete nutritional demands, additional protein sources must be added to the necessary carbohydrates and some protein included in these grains. Adding grains to the diet promotes overall nutrient availability and feed diversification.

Supplements of Protein

To address the greater protein needs of laying hens, protein supplements are essential in addition to grains. Rich in proteins, ingredients including fish meal, soybean meal, and blood meal are often utilized in layer feeds. These supplements aid in supplying chickens with enough protein for healthy growth and egg production.

Supplements with Phosphorus and Calcium

Since calcium is required for robust eggshells, it is an essential mineral for layers. Oyster shells and limestone are popular sources of extra calcium. As phosphorus and calcium operate together, phosphorus is often supplied via supplements such as dicalcium phosphate. Maintaining adequate concentrations of these minerals promotes bone health and helps avoid abnormalities in the eggshell.

Supplements of vitamins and minerals

To treat any possible deficiencies, extra vitamins and minerals may be given to chicken feed. A wide variety of vital nutrients may be supplied by adding multivitamins and mineral premixes. These supplements are especially helpful when the layers are unwell or stressed, or when the base feed is deficient in certain vitamins or minerals.

Feeding Plans And Administration
Creating a Schedule for Feeding

Establishing a regular feeding schedule is critical to the well-being and output of laying hens. For the purpose of establishing a pattern that will assist control their eating habits and general metabolism, layers should be fed at the same times every day. All hens will have equal access to the feed if it is provided in designated troughs or feeders, which will lessen competition and waste.

Modifying the Quantity and Quality of Feed

The chickens' age, weight, and stage of production should all be taken into consideration when determining how much feed is given. Layers may need more nutrition during peak egg production in order to maintain their energy levels and egg yield. Feed amount and quality may be changed as necessary with the support of routine body condition and egg production monitoring.

Controlling Feed Handling and Storage

Maintaining feed quality and avoiding spoiling requires using the right handling and storage techniques. To keep it safe from contamination, dampness, and pests, feed has to be kept in a cold, dry location. The nutritional content of the feed is preserved when it is stored in clean, sealed containers. Stale or tainted feed may be avoided by routinely checking feed storage facilities and switching the feedstock.

Feed Management System Implementation

Feed management systems may assist increase efficiency and simplify the feeding process. Examples of these systems include automatic feeders and monitoring systems. While monitoring systems are able to check feed consumption and identify any problems with feed supply or quality, automated feeders guarantee that layers get regular quantities of feed without the need for user intervention.

Taking Care of Typical Feeding Problems

Feed waste, unequal distribution, and nutritional imbalances are common feeding problems that need to be quickly resolved. To fix these problems and guarantee that the layers' nutritional demands are continuously satisfied, it is helpful to evaluate the feeding arrangement on a regular basis and seek advice from a poultry nutritionist.

CHAPTER SIX

Typical Poultry Illnesses And How To Avoid Them

Overview Of Poultry Illnesses

Taking care of birds that are prone to different illnesses is a big part of farming poultry, and it may have a big effect on the health, output, and overall profitability of the farm. For layer farming to be successful, it is essential to comprehend prevalent chicken illnesses and put preventative measures into practice.

bird flu

Viruses that infect chickens and cause severe respiratory distress, poor egg production, and high death rates are known as avian influenza or bird flu. Contact with contaminated feed, equipment, or diseased birds is often how it spreads. Preventive steps include keeping the surroundings tidy, preventing interaction with wild birds, and putting stringent biosecurity procedures in place.

Newcastle Illness

Another viral disease that affects poultry is Newcastle Disease, which manifests as coughing, discharge from the nose, and decreased egg production. This illness may cause large losses and spreads quickly. In addition to maintaining proper cleanliness and biosecurity, vaccinations are important preventative measures.

coccidiosis

Protozoa are the parasite infection that causes coccidiosis, which damages the intestines and stunts development. Diarrhea, weight loss, and decreased egg production are other symptoms. Using coccidiostats in feed, maintaining good sanitation, and controlling litter quality is also part of prevention.

Salmonella

Humans and birds may get very sick from salmonella infections in poultry. Lethargy, fever, and diarrhea are among the symptoms. Salmonella may be avoided by following stringent hygiene standards, managing rodent populations, and managing feed and water supply sanitization procedures.

Additional Common Illnesses

Poultry producers should also be mindful of the illnesses known as Infectious Bronchitis, Marek's Disease, and Fowl Pox. Every one of these illnesses has distinct signs and preventative measures, like as immunisation and better husbandry techniques.

In summary

It takes a complete strategy that includes immunization, good cleanliness, and close flock health monitoring to prevent common chicken illnesses. Farmers can safeguard their layers and guarantee the health and productivity of their flock by comprehending the signs and putting into practice efficient preventive measures.

Medication And Vaccination
The Value of Immunisation

An essential part of managing poultry health is vaccination. It aids in defending birds against a range of viral illnesses that might seriously harm their well-being and output. Maintaining flock health and controlling disease outbreaks need effective immunization regimens.

Vaccine Types

For poultry, there are several vaccination options available, such as recombinant, inactivated (killed), and live attenuated vaccines. Weakened virus strains used in live vaccinations elicit an immune response without actually spreading illness. Recombinant vaccines create immunity by genetic engineering, while inactivated vaccines employ dead pathogens to do so.

Schedule of Vaccinations

An efficient immunization regimen is essential for disease prevention. Layer hens are often vaccinated against Newcastle disease, Avian Influenza, and Marek's Disease. The particular vaccine and the age of the birds determine when and how often they should be vaccinated. It's crucial to adhere to the manufacturer's instructions and speak with a veterinarian to create a customized immunization schedule.

Drugs and Therapy

Medication may be needed in addition to vaccinations to control or cure certain illnesses. Antibiotics, antiparasitics, and antifungals are among the medications used to treat illnesses caused by bacteria, parasites, and fungi, respectively. To prevent resistance, it is important to administer drugs sparingly and in accordance with veterinarian advice.

Observation and Documentation

Maintaining precise documentation of immunization and drug regimens is essential for efficient health care. Maintaining current immunization records and keeping an eye out for any indications of disease are two important aspects of routine flock health monitoring that aid in quickly recognizing and treating health problems.

Medication and vaccination are essential for preserving the well-being and output of layer chickens. Farmers may efficiently manage and prevent infections in their flocks by adhering to a well-organized vaccination schedule, administering the right treatments, and maintaining thorough health records.

Using Biosecurity To Stop Outbreaks

Overview of Biosecurity

A collection of procedures known as "biosecurity" is intended to stop the entry and spread of illnesses within flocks of chickens. Ensuring food safety, safeguarding farm profitability, and preserving flock health all depend on effective biosecurity measures.

Physical Obstacles

Physical barriers that assist keep animals and unauthorized people out of chicken operations include fences and limited access zones. One of the main components of biosecurity is making sure that all entrance points are safe and that guests adhere to stringent hygiene guidelines.

Both hygiene and sanitation

To lower the danger of illness, it is essential to regularly clean and disinfect feed storage places, equipment, and poultry houses. To stop germs from spreading, this entails clearing out manure and other organic materials, cleaning surfaces, and providing footbaths for guests.

Management of Wildlife and Rodents

Poultry may get infections from wildlife and rodents. The danger of disease transmission is reduced by putting in place controls to keep animals out, such as secure feed storage and rodent control programs.

Keeping oneself clean and using protective gear.

Farm workers should maintain proper personal hygiene, which includes often washing their hands, changing into fresh clothes, and using protective gear such as boots and gloves. This aids in halting the spread of infections from one location to another.

Monitoring and Surveillance of Health

To identify any outbreaks early on, the flock must be regularly observed and its health monitored. This includes keeping track of any health concerns, regularly checking on the health of the birds, and watching for symptoms of sickness.

Strong biosecurity procedures must be put in place in order to stop disease outbreaks and guarantee the well-being of chicken flocks. Farmers may greatly lower the danger of illness and safeguard their layer farming operations by erecting physical barriers, keeping their surroundings clean, managing wildlife, and encouraging excellent personal hygiene.

CHAPTER SEVEN

Production And Handling Of Eggs

Knowing The Cycles Of Egg-Laying

It is essential to comprehend the chicken egg-laying cycle in order to produce eggs successfully. Because of their consistent cycles, layers—hens raised especially for their eggs—can help you better control their care and surroundings. A number of variables, including age, breed, diet, and environmental circumstances, may affect the egg-laying cycle.

crucial stages of the egg-laying process

1. Growth and Initial Laying

o Depending on the breed, hens often start producing eggs between 18 and 24 weeks of age. Usually smaller and fewer in number are the early eggs. This stage is essential for ensuring that chickens are getting enough food and are healthy enough to sustain their reproductive system.

2. Maximum Output

o Hens regularly lay eggs until they reach their peak production period, which typically occurs between 24 and 40 weeks. Hens produce around five to six eggs a week at this time, which is indicative of a high frequency of egg production. Hens remain healthy and productive throughout this time if they are properly managed.

3. Moult and Comeback

o Hens go through a molting period, when they develop new feathers and lose old ones, usually once a year. This time frame may momentarily impact egg production. Knowing the molt cycle makes it easier to prepare for and anticipate lower egg production.

Affecting Factors For Egg Production
1. Genetics and Breed

o The capacity of different breeds to produce eggs varies. Breeds with a reputation for producing large quantities of eggs include ISA Brown, Lohmann, and Hy-Line. It is easier to manage expectations and optimize circumstances for each breed when one is aware of breed-specific features.

2. Diet and Nutrition

o To sustain steady egg production, a balanced diet is essential. Layers' general health and egg development depend on a diet rich in protein, calcium, and other necessary elements. Formulating the optimal diet might be aided by consulting a poultry nutritionist.

3. surroundings

o A number of factors, including temperature, light exposure, and housing conditions, are important for egg production. Every day, hens need between 14 and 16 hours of light to maintain their ideal laying rates. Having suitable accommodation contributes to a decrease in stress and an increase in productivity.

Gathering And Treating Eggs
The Best Methods for Gathering Eggs

1. Prompt Acquisition

o Gather eggs at least twice a day to reduce the possibility of contamination and breakage. Regular gathering lowers the chance that the chickens will eat the eggs and keeps them from becoming dirty.

2. mild handling

• Take care while handling eggs to prevent damage and cracks. To gather eggs, use clean, dry hands or instruments. Eggs should not be dropped or handled roughly since this might cause damage or contamination.

Tools And Methods For Gathering Eggs
1. Using Spotless Containers

o Keep gathered eggs in dry, clean containers. To avoid contamination, never use containers that have previously contained food or other things. It is advised to use specialized egg cartons or trays made for chicken eggs.

2. Keeping Things Tidy

To avoid the entry of microorganisms, make sure that collecting sites and equipment are maintained hygienic and clean. Keep all locations where eggs are handled and egg collecting containers clean and sterilized on a regular basis.

Managing Procedures to Guarantee Quality

1. Steer Clear of Egg Contact with Unclean Surfaces

o Eggs must not be exposed to excessive dampness or come into touch with unclean surfaces. Maintaining the cleanliness of instruments and collecting places contributes to the preservation of egg quality.

2. Examining Eggs to Ensure Quality

o Examine each egg for abnormalities, dirt, or breaks as it is being collected. To guarantee that only eggs of the highest caliber reach customers, throw away any eggs that are dirty or broken.

Storage As Well As Quality Assurance
Appropriate Strategies for Storing Eggs

1. Control of Temperature

o To preserve freshness, store eggs at a constant 50–60°F (10–15°C) temperature. Steer clear of temperature swings since these may impair the eggs' quality and shelf life. In business settings, refrigeration is often employed to prolong freshness.

2. Controlling Humidity

o To keep eggs from losing moisture, keep storage facilities at the right humidity levels. Eggs may become too wet in high-humidity conditions, whereas excessive moisture loss may occur in low-humidity conditions. Humidity levels should ideally range from 70 to 75%.

Measures of Quality Control

1. Frequent Inspections of Quality

o Conduct routine quality tests to make sure eggs meet requirements for freshness and safety. This involves keeping an eye out for any indications of spoiling, such as strange scents or unusual looks. Candling may be used to find anomalies or flaws inside.

2. Egg Categorisation and Grading

o Sort eggs according to their size and quality. Grades A, B, and C are common categories.

Appropriate grading aids in upholding quality standards and fulfilling market demands.

Avoiding and Resolving Quality Problems

1. Handling the Risk of Contamination

• Put precautions in place to avoid contamination, such as keeping storage spaces clean and making sure that appropriate hygiene procedures are followed. Maintain regular sanitation and cleaning of storage facilities and equipment.

2. Transport and Handling

• Take extra care while handling eggs in transit to avoid breaking them. To preserve quality, make sure eggs are transported in controlled environments and use the proper packing materials.

CHAPTER EIGHT

Preserving The Welfare Of Poultry

Keeping chickens happy is essential to layer farming since it has a direct impact on the quantity, quality, and general health of the flock. Hens living in a cozy and healthful environment are certain to be productive as well, thanks to good management techniques. The main facets of poultry welfare are covered in this part, including stress and injury management, environmental enrichment, and behavior and health monitoring.

Keeping An Eye On Behavior And Health

Frequent Medical Exams

To keep your flock healthy and stop illness outbreaks, regular health examinations are crucial. Start by looking for any indications of disease or pain in your chickens every day.

Keep an eye out for physical signs like altered comb color, strange droppings, and changes in the quality of the feathers. Establish a regimen for deworming and immunizations to guard against common illnesses that affect chickens. Keeping a health record for every bird might assist in monitoring any problems and guarantee prompt attention.

Observations of Behaviour

Monitoring behavior is just as important as doing physical examinations. Keep an eye out for unusual behavior in your hens, such as hostility, feather pecking, or lethargy. Pheasants in good health usually have normal behaviors such as dust-bathing and foraging, and they are also gregarious and energetic. Behavior changes may be a sign of stress, disease, or pain. To address any possible problems, note any changes in behavior and, if necessary, get advice from a veterinarian.

Early Disease Detection

Early illness identification helps stop illnesses from spreading across the flock. Learn about common illnesses that affect chickens and their symptoms, such as respiratory problems, digestive problems, or parasite infections. Implement biosecurity measures, such as regulated access to poultry areas and good sanitation standards, to avoid the entry of illness. The general health of the flock depends on routine health examinations and timely care of ill birds.

Bringing In Environmental Enhancement

Room & Accommodation

The well-being of laying hens depends critically on having enough room. Make sure the housing for your poultry has enough room for each bird to walk around comfortably, as well as areas for sleeping, dust-bathing, and foraging. In addition to increasing the danger of disease transmission, overcrowding may cause stress and violence. Include distinct spaces in your chicken building for diverse purposes, such as feeding stations, roosting perches, and nesting boxes.

Possibilities for Nesting and Foraging

For chickens to be healthy, chances for natural behaviors like foraging and nesting must be provided. Add elements where the hens may peck and search for food, such as scratch mats or places covered with litter. To promote natural nesting behavior, make sure that nesting boxes are placed in conveniently accessible locations and have clean bedding within. Giving the birds access to outside runways or hanging veggies are examples of enrichment activities that may improve their quality of life.

Lighting and Ventilation

Ensuring that your chickens are kept in a pleasant environment requires proper lighting and ventilation. Make sure there is enough ventilation in your home to avoid the accumulation of ammonia and moisture, both of which may cause respiratory issues. Enough illumination should be provided to control the hens' laying cycles, but there should also be times when it is dark to replicate the outdoors and encourage sound sleep.

Handling Injuries And Stress
Recognizing and Mitigating Stressors

Maintaining the well-being of chickens requires identifying and minimizing stresses. Overcrowding, inadequate nutrition, and abrupt environmental changes are examples of common stresses. Reduce sudden changes to the flock's surroundings and establish a pattern for management that is stable. To lessen stress and rivalry among birds, make sure that feeding and watering systems are dependable and easily available.

Taking Care of Sickness and Injuries

It's critical to treat wounds and diseases as soon as possible to avoid consequences and maintain your flock's health. Establish procedures for managing sick or wounded birds, such as separating them from the main flock to stop the spread of illness. In accordance with a veterinarian's instructions, provide the proper care and assistance, such as medicine or wound care. Check your poultry often for any indications of injuries or health problems, and respond appropriately.

Encouraging a Peaceful Environment

For the wellness of chickens, a peaceful and stress-free environment is essential. Reduce the amount of noise, jerky movements, and other disruptions that can make your hens nervous. Stress may be decreased and the general health of the flock can be enhanced by teaching employees how to handle birds gently and using low-stress handling methods. An environment that is well-maintained and enrichment activities implemented may also help create a flock that is healthier and more at ease.

CHAPTER NINE

Sanitation And Waste Management In Layer Farming Of Poultry

Techniques For Discarding Waste

For a chicken layer farm to remain healthy and productive, efficient waste disposal is essential. If waste is not adequately handled, it may provide a breeding habitat for diseases, including manure and feed residues. This is a thorough overview of several waste disposal techniques that work well for chicken farms.

1. Landfill Disposal in Direct Form

One of the easiest ways is to just dispose of chicken waste in landfills, however, this isn't always the most environmentally friendly option. With this technique, garbage is moved to a specified landfill location and buried there. Although this method separates trash from farming activities well, there are environmental ramifications, including the possibility of fertilizer leakage into groundwater. Before choosing this approach, it is important to review environmental rules and local restrictions.

2. Application for Land

Spreading chicken dung directly onto agricultural fields is known as land application. Because it replenishes the soil with nutrients, this technique may improve soil fertility. To prevent over-application, which may result in nutrient runoff and water contamination, cautious management is necessary. To protect the environment and optimize nutrient utilization, farmers should apply manure after taking into account many elements, including soil type, crop requirements, and meteorological conditions.

3. Systems for Manure Management

Poultry dung may be converted into compost and biogas using sophisticated manure management technologies like anaerobic digesters. By breaking down organic waste without the presence of oxygen, anaerobic digestion creates compost that may be added to soil and biogas that can be used as a source of energy. This approach is sustainable for large-scale poultry farms since it lowers waste volume and offers a substitute energy source.

4. Burning

Poultry waste is incinerated, or burned at high temperatures until it turns to ash. This technique works well to destroy pathogens and reduce volume, but it uses a lot of energy. Certain wastes, such as ill birds or hazardous materials, are often burned. For the purpose of controlling pollutants and upholding environmental laws, appropriate emissions control systems must be installed.

5. Vermicomposting

Poultry manure is broken down into nutrient-rich compost by the employment of earthworms in vermicomposting. This process creates high-quality compost that may improve soil health while being kind to the environment. On the farm, vermicomposting devices may be installed to process waste continuously and lessen the need for outside waste disposal. Recycling waste materials also helps to create a circular agricultural system.

Facilities Cleaning And Disinfection

Keeping the surroundings clean and sterile is essential to keeping chickens healthy and free from illness. Poultry housing and equipment should be cleaned and disinfected on a regular basis to lower the risk of infection and increase farm output. Here's a thorough look at the cleaning and disinfection techniques required for good sanitation.

1. Standard Cleaning Techniques

Clearing of visible trash and debris from poultry facilities is part of routine cleaning. This includes cleaning and sweeping the floors, walls, and equipment to get rid of impurities such as feed spills and manure. Daily or weekly cleaning schedules should be established, based on the facility's size and the quantity of birds present. To guarantee the complete removal of organic waste and to prepare surfaces for disinfection, use the proper cleaning supplies and tools.

2. Methods of Disinfection

After cleaning, disinfection is essential to get rid of germs and pathogens. Depending on the particular requirements of the facility, a variety of disinfectants, including phenolic compounds, chlorine-based solutions, and quaternary ammonium compounds, might be utilized. To guarantee efficacy, it's essential to adhere to the manufacturer's recommendations regarding dilution and contact time. All surfaces, including floors, walls, ceilings, and equipment, should be thoroughly disinfected.

3. Equipment Sanitisation

It's critical to sanitize poultry equipment, including nesting boxes, waterers, and feeders, to stop the spread of illness. It is necessary to properly clean the equipment before disinfecting it. After removing residues using brushes, scrapers, and high-pressure water jets, apply the proper disinfectants. To guarantee appropriate operation and cleanliness, equipment must undergo routine maintenance and inspections.

4

. Management of Air Quality

One part of facility cleaning that is sometimes disregarded is air quality control. Reducing moisture and ammonia levels, which may aggravate respiratory problems in chickens, requires proper ventilation. A healthy atmosphere is contributed to by routine maintenance and inspection of ventilation systems, which include fans and ducting. Air sanitizers and appropriate ventilation are other tools for controlling airborne infections.

5. Measures for Biosecurity

It is possible to stop the entrance and spread of illnesses by including biosecurity measures in routines for cleaning and disinfection. This includes using footbaths for workers entering the plant, employing protective apparel, and limiting access to sections housing poultry. Upholding strict cleaning and disinfection procedures is essential for keeping hygienic standards high.

Recycling And Composting Trash

Poultry waste may be recycled and composted, which are environmentally friendly methods that also increase farm output. These techniques not only efficiently handle trash but also provide important resources for improving soil quality. This is a thorough guide on recycling and composting chicken manure.

1. Fundamentals of Composting

The act of turning organic material, like chicken dung, into nutrient-rich compost is called composting. In order to provide the ideal environment for microbial activity, trash is mixed with carbon-rich materials, such as wood chips or straw, during the composting process. Turning compost heaps on a regular basis will guarantee uniform decomposition and aeration. For composting to be effective, the right temperature and moisture content must be maintained.

2. Composting System Types

Poultry farms may use a variety of composting techniques, including in-vessel systems, windrows, and static heaps. Making large mounds of composting material and turning them on a regular basis is known as a static pile. Using specialized equipment, windrow composting entails creating lengthy rows of composting material that are rotated on a regular basis. Enclosed composting units that provide regulated conditions for decomposition are known as in-vessel systems. The size of the operation and the resources available determine the system to use.

3. Reusing Chicken Waste

Recycling poultry waste entails turning it into useful goods like soil amendments or animal feed. If pathogens are removed, processed chicken dung may be used as a source of protein in animal feed. Poultry waste may also be repurposed to create biochar, a kind of charcoal that increases soil fertility. Recycling increases the value of byproducts while also reducing the amount of garbage produced.

4. Advantages for the Environment

Poultry waste composting and recycling have a positive impact on the environment. These methods minimize land usage and cut down on greenhouse gas emissions by keeping garbage out of landfills. By adding organic matter and minerals, composting also strengthens the soil's structure and ability to hold water. Recycling helps to promote sustainable agricultural methods by lowering the demand for synthetic fertilizers.

5. Obstacles and Things to Think About

Recycling and composting have advantages, but they can have drawbacks. In order to prevent problems like smell, leachate, and insect attraction, proper management is necessary. Farmers are responsible for making sure that recycling and composting procedures follow local laws and ordinances. To ensure effective installation and operation, training and education on best practices are necessary.

CHAPTER TEN

Putting Your Eggs On The Market And Selling Them

Finding The Right Target Markets

For your poultry layer farming business to be successful, you must have a clear understanding of your target market. Determine who your prospective clients are first. Local eateries, farmers' markets, grocery shops,

and individual customers may all fall under this category. Every market group has distinct requirements and shopping habits.

Local grocery stores: If you can provide fresh, high-quality eggs, they will likely be your regular customers. To build rapport, provide shop managers with samples and details about your agricultural methods.

Restaurants: Using fresh eggs may be a fantastic selling factor, and many restaurants are interested in using items that are obtained locally. Go for eateries that highlight fresh ingredients or farm-to-table cuisine.

Farmers' Markets: Direct sales to consumers work best at farmers' markets. Customers at these marketplaces often seek fresh, organic, and locally grown goods.

Establishing a booth and engaging with consumers face-to-face may foster brand loyalty and provide quick feedback.

Individual Customers: You may develop a devoted clientele by selling directly to customers.

Think about launching a subscription business that provides clients with a steady supply of eggs. By doing this, you may create a steady revenue stream and guarantee steady sales.

Subheadings:

1. Investigating Market Needs: To learn about the preferences and needs of prospective customers, and conduct surveys or interviews with them. You may successfully address their wants by customizing your marketing plan with the use of this information.

2. Analysing Competition: Find out who else in the area produces eggs. Recognize their product offers, price, and marketing tactics. This will assist you in finding a market niche and differentiating your items.

3. Creating Buyer Personas: Describe your prospective clients in-depth, taking into account their interests, purchasing patterns, and demographics. This will enable you to more successfully target your marketing campaigns.

4. Developing Relationships: Make a solid rapport with your purchasers. Trust will be established and repeat business will be

encouraged with regular contact and high-quality items.

5. Investigating New Markets: As your company develops, think about branching out into other areas or markets. To maintain your company's competitiveness, investigate new trends and commercial prospects.

Strategies For Pricing

Setting a competitive price for your eggs is essential to drawing in clients and making a profit. Pricing is determined by a number of variables, such as market demand, competition, and manufacturing costs.

Cost analysis: Start by figuring out how much it costs to produce a certain amount of feed, labor, housing, and other supplies. Having a clear understanding of your costs will enable you to establish pricing that both pays for your outlays and leaves a profit.

Market research: Find out how much eggs cost at your neighborhood market. Think about the costs associated with various providers and egg varieties, including free-range or organic. This will assist you in setting your prices in a competitive market.

Value Proposition: Stress the special features of your eggs, including their quality, freshness, or the surroundings in which your chickens are kept. This may be sufficient to support a higher cost than for regular eggs.

Discounts and Promotions: To draw in new clients or promote large purchases, think about implementing discounts or promotions. Offer a loyalty program or a discount to customers who are repeat consumers, for instance.

Subheadings:

1. Recognising Cost Structures: List all of the expenses related to producing eggs, including

feed, maintenance, and utilities. You may use this to establish a starting price for your eggs.

2. Competitive Pricing Analysis: Research your rivals' pricing tactics. Recognize their egg pricing strategy and modify your own to provide a competitive value.

3. Seasonal Price Adjustment: Supply and demand may cause price changes. To stay profitable, think about changing your rates throughout the busiest and slowest times of the year.

4. Providing Value-Added Products: Look at ways to add value, such as organic certification or distinctive packaging, to support higher pricing and draw in upscale clients.

5. Monitoring and Modifying Prices: Continually assess your pricing plan in light of shifting production costs, consumer input, and market trends. Be adaptable and prepared to change course as necessary.

Distribution And Packaging

Maintaining the quality of your eggs and making sure they reach your consumers in excellent condition depends on efficient packing and delivery. Effective packaging is important for marketing and branding as well.

Packaging: Select packaging that is aesthetically pleasing and protects the eggs during transportation. The use of sturdy containers that provide an excellent view of the eggs is something to think about. Customers who care about the environment may also be drawn to eco-friendly packaging solutions.

Labeling: Make sure your packaging has legible labels with all the pertinent information on it, like nutritional facts, expiry dates, and your farm's name. Effective labeling may increase the attractiveness and credibility of your goods.

Distribution methods: Choose the methods that will distribute your eggs to consumers most effectively. This might include working with nearby companies, using local distribution networks, or making direct deliveries.

Organize your logistics to guarantee the prompt and secure delivery of your eggs. This includes arranging for delivery, keeping track of stock, and making sure that eggs are stored properly to preserve their freshness.

Subheadings:

1. Choosing the Best Packaging Materials: Investigate various packaging materials and choose those that provide protection, preserve freshness, and complement your brand's core values.

2. Creating Decorative Labels: Create labels that are both visually appealing and useful. Make sure your brand identity is prominent while including all pertinent information.

3. Putting Together an Effective Distribution Strategy: Create a distribution strategy that addresses the practicalities of transporting your eggs safely and effectively from the farm to the consumer.

4. Maintaining Quality Control: Take steps to ensure that eggs are in good condition both before and after they are packaged and distributed. This entails keeping an eye on handling procedures and storage conditions.

5. Creating a Distribution Network: To increase your reach, think about forming alliances with regional distributors or merchants. Creating a dependable network may facilitate distribution and boost market share.

CHAPTER ELEVEN

Developing And Growing Your Farm

Making Growth Plans
Evaluating Present-Day Farm Activities

It's critical to do a comprehensive evaluation of your present operations before pursuing growth. Examining flock performance, feed efficiency, egg production rates, and general farm management are all included in this. You may determine the strengths and opportunities for improvement on your farm by analyzing these indicators. To predict how expansion could affect these aspects and identify possible obstacles, think about using performance data.

Clearly Defined Expansion Objectives

Clearly state your goals for the growth. Do you want to expand into new markets, provide a wider range of products, or produce more eggs? Establishing quantifiable, unambiguous goals can direct your growth plan and keep you focused on your aims. Achieving a given number of layers, increasing manufacturing efficiency, or hitting certain income objectives are a few examples of goals.

Budgeting And Financial Planning

Large financial resources are needed for expansion. Make a thorough financial strategy that accounts for the price of increased labor, equipment, and new facilities. Determine possible ROIs and create a budget that accounts for both anticipated and unforeseen costs. Seek the advice of a financial professional to make sure your strategy is workable and long-term.

Regulatory Aspects to Take into Account

Find out about local laws pertaining to the growth and farming of chicken. Zoning rules, environmental restrictions, and requirements for animal care are a few examples of this. It is essential to adhere to these standards in order to prevent legal complications and possible penalties. To learn about all the criteria, speak with agricultural experts or the local government.

Hazard Assessment

Determine the possible dangers of growing, such as disease outbreaks, changes in the market, or interruptions to the supply chain. Create risk management measures, such as insurance policies and backup plans, to help reduce these risks. You may efficiently handle obstacles by evaluating and upgrading these tactics on a regular basis.

Including New Equipment And Facilities

Evaluating Facility Requirements

Determine, in light of your growth ambitions, the kind and extent of additional facilities that are needed. This might include more henhouses, structures for storing feed, or spaces for processing eggs. To make sure the new facilities suit your operating demands, take into account elements like ventilation, lighting, and space requirements.

Choosing Equipment

Invest in machinery that increases output and effectiveness. This might include temperature control systems, robotic egg collectors, and automated feeding systems. Look into the newest equipment and technology possibilities to discover solutions that meet the unique needs of your farm.

Planning and Building

Collaborate with farm planners or architects to create efficient and practical facilities. The layout should make managing your flock easier and fit its demands. Keep an eye on the building process to make sure it adheres to quality standards and is finished on schedule and within budget.

Including New Facilities

Make a plan for incorporating new facilities into your current farming activities. This includes planning the logistics of shifting equipment, educating employees on new platforms, and making sure the changeover goes well. Create an integration process timetable and make sure your staff is aware of it.

Upkeep And Improvements

Long-term success depends on new facilities and equipment receiving regular upkeep. Schedule regular maintenance and set aside funds for upgrades and repairs. Maintaining your facilities in a proactive manner can assist keep them operating smoothly and help avoid malfunctions.

Overseeing Bigger Flocks And Activities

personnel and instruction

You'll need more workers as your farm grows in order to oversee bigger flocks and activities. Employ someone with a background in raising chickens or provide new staff training. Provide training courses including animal care, safety procedures, and farm management techniques.

efficiency of operations

Put in place mechanisms to improve operational effectiveness. This might include optimizing feed and water distribution, automating repetitive operations, or employing software for flock management. Evaluate your operations on a regular basis and look for methods to save expenses on labor and simplify procedures.

Biosecurity and Health

It's critical to maintain flock health, particularly when there are more birds involved. Put strong biosecurity measures in place to stop disease outbreaks, including limiting access to the farm, cleaning and disinfecting equipment, and routinely checking the health of the flock. Create a health management plan in collaboration with a veterinarian, and act quickly to address any health concerns.

Production Supervision

Keep a tight eye on production indicators to make sure your growth is fulfilling expectations. Monitor feed conversion ratios, egg production rates, and flock performance as a whole. Make educated judgments on management procedures using this data, and modify your plans as necessary.

Relationships with Customers and Market Growth

Develop connections with possible clients and look into new markets as your manufacturing capacity increases. Create a marketing plan to highlight your enlarged business and set your items apart. To expand your market presence, go to industry events, connect with other manufacturers, and become involved in the community.

Conclusion

Accepting Layer Farming for Poultry

As we draw to a close our introduction to poultry layer farming tutorial, it's important to consider the lessons learned and advice that will help you succeed in this fulfilling industry. For those who are interested in agriculture and animal husbandry, poultry layer farming presents a great prospect with its emphasis on egg production.

Knowing the Fundamentals

The foundation of poultry layer farming is a firm grasp of the fundamentals, including management, housing, food, and breeds. It is essential to understand the various layer breeds and the requirements that each one has in order to maximize egg production and preserve flock health. For novices, it might be a good idea to begin with a modest number of hens and then progressively increase as expertise grows.

Developing Appropriate Infrastructure

Purchasing appropriate housing and equipment is another essential component of a profitable layer farm for chickens. To keep themselves safe from illnesses and predators, layers need housing that is well-ventilated, clean, and secure. To maximize egg production, nesting places must have enough room, enough illumination, and appropriate conditions. Balanced food and clean water availability will also make a big difference in the general well-being and output of your flock.

Taking Care of Your Nutrition and Health

Layer farming of chicken depends heavily on diet and health management. Maintaining the health and productivity of your flock may be achieved via routine health checks, vaccines, and biosecurity measures that assist prevent and manage infections. Optimal egg production and general well-being may be supported by feeding laying hens a balanced diet that satisfies their nutritional requirements.

Record-keeping and financial planning

For your chicken layer farming business to be successful over the long run, you must have sound financial planning and record-keeping practices. You can track the profitability of your business and make wise choices by keeping thorough records of your costs, output, and money. A successful and sustainable business will also benefit from planning for future investments and accounting for unforeseen expenses.

Ongoing Education and Adjustment

Eventually, the secret to success in chicken layer farming is constant learning and adapting. Keep up with the most recent developments in feed formulations, disease control strategies, and poultry management. Engaging in networking activities with other poultry farmers, going to seminars, and consulting with professionals may provide significant perspectives and assistance while negotiating the obstacles and prospects within this industry.

In conclusion, for novices prepared to put in the time and effort to properly comprehend and manage their flocks, layer farming provides a rewarding and possibly profitable option. You may create a productive chicken layer farm that produces fresh eggs and advances your larger agricultural objectives by putting an emphasis on sound planning, management, and ongoing learning.

Beginner's Guide To Poultry Layer Farming: Important Things To Know

Beginning a Poultry Layer Farming Enterprise

Establishing a layer farm for chickens requires a few key procedures. Start by learning about the many laying hen breeds and selecting the one that best fits your agricultural objectives. The Rhode Island Red and White Leghorn are popular breeds for novices because of their great egg production and versatility. Comprehending the distinct requirements and attributes of your preferred breed will enable you to provide optimal care and maximize the production of eggs.

Configuring the Housing for Poultry

For the health and production of your laying hens, you must provide the perfect atmosphere.

The housing has to be dry, protected from predators, and well-ventilated. Take into account elements like nesting boxes, illumination, and the amount of space needed.

In the coop, a hen usually needs 1.5 to 2 square feet of room. In order to control temperature and humidity, which may impact egg quality and hen health, proper ventilation is essential.

Nutrition and Feeding

For laying hens to be healthy and productive, their food must be balanced. Give laying hens commercial layer feed that is specially designed to suit their nutritional demands. The proper ratio of proteins, vitamins, and minerals should be present in this diet to promote both egg production and general health. You may improve their nutrition even more by adding fresh fruits and vegetables to their diet, as well as calcium-rich foods like oyster shells.

Medical Administration

It takes frequent attention to a number of aspects, like as illness prevention and management, to maintain the health of your flock. Establish a vaccination program and use strong biosecurity protocols to stop the spread of illnesses. Keep an eye out for symptoms of disease in your hens, such as decreased egg production or behavioral abnormalities, and seek veterinary advice when necessary.

Maintaining Documents and Managing Finances

Maintaining accurate records is essential to running a profitable layer farm for chickens. Maintain thorough records of your spending, health problems, feed usage, and egg production. You may use this information to manage expenses, keep tabs on your flock's performance, and make well-informed judgments regarding your farming methods.

You can secure the sustainability of your business and efficient resource management by creating a financial strategy and budget.

Growth and Extension

As you have more expertise in layering chickens, you could think about growing your business. This might include getting more chickens, buying more equipment, or looking into new markets for your eggs. To guarantee that you can continue to provide the high standard of care and supervision that your hens need, carefully consider any additions. To sum up, meticulous preparation, commitment, and a readiness to learn are necessary when beginning a layer farm for chicken. Beginners may establish a profitable chicken layer farm that supplies fresh eggs and fulfills their agricultural goals by concentrating on appropriate breed selection, housing, nutrition, health management, and financial planning.

THE END

Made in the USA
Columbia, SC
10 March 2025